Book of Sayings

PETA ZAFIR

Book of Sayings

Book 5

©2022 Peta Zafir

All rights reserved.

No part of this book may be reproduced in any form or by any electronic or mechanical means, including information storage and retrieval systems, without written permission from the author, except in the case of a reviewer, who may quote brief passages embodied in critical articles or in a review.

Trademarked names appear throughout this book. Rather than use a trademark symbol with every occurrence of a trademarked name, names are used in an editorial fashion, with no intention of infringement of the respective owner's trademark.

The information in this book is distributed on an "as is" basis, without warranty. Although every precaution has been taken in the preparation of this work, neither the author nor the publisher shall have any liability to any person or entity with respect to any loss or damage caused or alleged to be caused directly or indirectly by the information contained in this book.

Peta Zafir Publishing
www.petazafir.com

ISBN 978-0-6452140-7-9

Peta Zafir Publishing
www.petazafir.com
Peta Zafir You Tube Channel

BOOKS BY PETA ZAFIR
Health in Poetry Book 1
Health in Poetry Book 2
Book of Sayings Book 1
Book of Sayings Book 2
Book of Sayings Book 3
Book of Sayings Book 4
Book of Sayings Book 5
Book of Sayings Book 6
Scenar For Beginners
Book of Sayings Book 1 in Italian

All books are available in print and eBook format from:
www.petazafir.com/books

Dedication

I dedicate this book to Stefano Palumbo whom has been a wonderful source of encouragement and support throughout my writing processes and who translated my *Book of Sayings Book 1,* which made it possible to reach a wider range of readers.

Book of Sayings   Book 5

One needs to find
Time to see Friends
Hope to move forward
Happiness to enjoy Life and
Wisdom to understand your Path

Book of Sayings   Book 5

Go Natural,
Be Informed,
You Decide,
Get Outcomes

Book of Sayings   Book 5

The only way to change your life is to take a step

Book of Sayings   Book 5

Don't give your life away

Live it as you want it to be

Book of Sayings   Book 5

Fear places us on the incorrect path
Live in strength and courage

Book of Sayings   Book 5

To find happiness, fulfilment and
your Path
You need first to find yourself

Book of Sayings   Book 5

I cannot change the past, however
I am the master of my Present
Creating my Future

Consistency is the winner
NOT perfection

Book of Sayings   Book 5

Move forward every day,
Sometimes only in little steps and
On other days, large strides

Book of Sayings   Book 5

Prepare for the Future

And

Live in the Present

Book of Sayings   Book 5

Permanent change is a slow journey
It requires awareness, adaption and courage

Book of Sayings   Book 5

Today let gratitude in and feel the
Blessings of what you have

Book of Sayings   Book 5

Don't wallow in self-pity
Stand up and take a strong step forward

Book of Sayings   Book 5

If you are not happy where you are
Change Direction and Reactions

Book of Sayings   Book 5

Bring Happiness and Joy into your Life
Through Change, Focus &
Being Proactive

Book of Sayings   Book 5

Life is a Journey

What is your next Adventure

Book of Sayings   Book 5

Babies and Children live in the present

Ignite your inner child and

Live just for today

Book of Sayings   Book 5

Today you begin
your incredible life journey

Book of Sayings   Book 5

Go back to Basics:

Clean your surrounding

Minimize your things

Utilize your time well

Focus on Yourself

You are important

Book of Sayings   Book 5

Remember:
If it is meant to be
Then it will come to me

Book of Sayings   Book 5

From trauma and collapse
Begins understanding and growth

Book of Sayings   Book 5

Regardless of your Starting Point
Just Keep Walking Forward

Book of Sayings   Book 5

Don't let the fear of Failure
Stop you Today

BOOK OF SAYINGS   BOOK 5

Walk into each new Day
Trust yourself and make Life Happen

Book of Sayings   Book 5

Changing one person at a time
Changes the world

Book of Sayings   Book 5

Growth is necessary for
Change to occur

Book of Sayings   Book 5

I perceive myself as I am
Strive for my ideal and
Realize my human limitations

Book of Sayings   Book 5

Peace is the answer

Book of Sayings   Book 5

Change only occurs when you
Take a step into the unknown

Book of Sayings   Book 5

I now start the work to be the best ME I can be

Book of Sayings   Book 5

If you don't become part of the fight
Be prepared to Live in the outcome

Book of Sayings   Book 5

You may not be thinking about Life
However, Life is thinking about you

Book of Sayings   Book 5

Chose the kind of human being you want to be

Then be that person

Book of Sayings   Book 5

Never stop Learning
Expand your Development
Through Continued Learning

Book of Sayings   Book 5

Do not define yourself by comparing and competing with others

Book of Sayings   Book 5

Conformity may appear comfortable

However never lose yourself

Fear is an indicator that something in your life needs Action

Book of Sayings   Book 5

Your body will Heal Itself
With a little Help and Nurturing

Book of Sayings   Book 5

Give Yourself Permission to
Stop, Calm and just Be

Stop filling your Life in, and
Start living your Life fully

Peta Zafir Publishing
www.petazafir.com
Peta Zafir You Tube Channel

BOOKS BY PETA ZAFIR

Health in Poetry Book 1
Health in Poetry Book 2
Book of Sayings Book 1
Book of Sayings Book 2
Book of Sayings Book 3
Book of Sayings Book 4
Book of Sayings Book 5
Book of Sayings Book 6
Scenar For Beginners
Book of Sayings Book 1 in Italian

All books are available in print and eBook format from:
www.petazafir.com/books

www.ingramcontent.com/pod-product-compliance
Lightning Source LLC
Chambersburg PA
CBHW071836290426
44109CB00017B/1831